CLASSY CLIMB PLANNER

Name: _____

Email: _____

Copyright © 2019 Ericka S. Williams. All rights reserved.
Published by The Classy Climb
ISBN 978-1-73420-820-7

All rights reserved, including the right to reproduce this book or portions thereof in any form whatsoever. For information, address the publisher.

   All rights reserved. This book or parts thereof may not be reproduced in any form, stored in any retrieval system, or transmitted in any form by any means—electronic, mechanical, photocopy, recording, or otherwise—without prior written permission of the publisher, except as provided by United States of America copyright law.

FOR THE ACTION TAKERS

The purpose of this planner is to get traction in your goals this year. The way to get traction is writing down daily your microgoals and evaluating yourself. Not to beat yourself up, but to see the growth and overall change.

I took the tactics I do myself daily and sharing it with you.
I want you add gratitude, action and new accountability to your life.

-Ericka S. Williams

BIG PICTURE

IMAGINE 90 DAYS HAVE PASSED AND YOU'VE ACOMPLISHED YOUR GOALS, WRITE OUT HOW YOUR LIFE LOOKS LIKE NOW.

" Your network is your net worth!"

WRITE DOWN 150 PEOPLE YOU KNOW

1. ___
2. ___
3. ___
4. ___
5. ___
6. ___
7. ___
8. ___
9. ___
10. ___
11. ___
12. ___
13. ___
14. ___
15. ___
16. ___
17. ___
18. ___
19. ___
20. ___
21. ___
22. ___
23. ___
24. ___
25. ___
26. ___
27. ___
28. ___
29. ___
30. ___
31. ___
32. ___
33. ___
34. ___
35. ___
36. ___
37. ___
38. ___
39. ___
40. ___
41. ___
42. ___
43. ___
44. ___
45. ___
46. ___
47. ___
48. ___
49. ___
50. ___
51. ___
52. ___
53. ___
54. ___
55. ___
56. ___
57. ___
58. ___
59. ___
60. ___
61. ___
62. ___
63. ___
64. ___
65. ___
66. ___
67. ___
68. ___
69. ___
70. ___
71. ___
72. ___
73. ___
74. ___
75. ___
76. ___
77. ___
78. ___
79. ___
80. ___
81. ___
82. ___
83. ___
84. ___
85. ___
86. ___
87. ___
88. ___
89. ___
90. ___
91. ___
92. ___
93. ___
94. ___
95. ___
96. ___
97. ___
98. ___
99. ___
100. ___
101. ___
102. ___
103. ___
104. ___
105. ___
106. ___
107. ___
108. ___
109. ___
110. ___
111. ___
112. ___
113. ___
114. ___
115. ___
116. ___
117. ___
118. ___
119. ___
120. ___
121. ___
122. ___
123. ___
124. ___
125. ___
126. ___
127. ___
128. ___
129. ___
130. ___
131. ___
132. ___
133. ___
134. ___
135. ___
136. ___
137. ___
138. ___
136. ___
137. ___
138. ___
139. ___
140. ___
141. ___
142. ___
143. ___
144. ___
145. ___
146. ___
147. ___
148. ___
149. ___
150. ___

HOW DO YOU WANT YOUR CONTACT LIST TO CHANGE GROW OR IMPROVE WITHIN THE NEXT 90 DAYS?

MONDAY

DATE : ____ ____ ___

" The best way to predict the future is to create it. "
-Peter Drucker

WHAT'S ONE THING YOU'RE GRATEFUL FOR?
_____
_____
_____

LIST 3 MICRO GOALS YOU CAN TACKLE TODAY

1. _____
MICRO GOAL
_____
_____
_____
_____

2. _____
MICRO GOAL
_____
_____
_____
_____

3. _____
MICRO GOAL
_____
_____
_____
_____

BIG WINS / LESSONS

DAY 1

REFLECTION

DID YOU GET SOME OF YOUR GOALS ACCOMPLISHED TODAY?
_____
_____
_____
_____
_____
_____
_____
_____
_____

HEALTH CHECK

HOW MANY CUPS OF WATER DID YOU DRINK?

☐ YES ☐ NO

DID YOU EXERCISE TODAY?
(a 15-20 min. walk counts)

WHAT ARE YOU THE MOST PROUD OF TODAY?

TUESDAY

DATE : ____ ____ ___

WHAT'S ONE THING YOU'RE GRATEFUL FOR?

_____
_____
_____

> "Difficulties are meant to rouse, not discourage."
> —William Ellery Channing, minister and psychologist

LIST 3 MICRO GOALS YOU CAN TACKLE TODAY

1. _____
MICRO GOAL
_____
_____
_____
_____

2. _____
MICRO GOAL
_____
_____
_____
_____

3. _____
MICRO GOAL
_____
_____
_____
_____

BIG WINS / LESSONS

```
┌────────────────────────────────────────────┐
│                                            │
│                                            │
│                                            │
│                                            │
│                                            │
└────────────────────────────────────────────┘
```

DAY 2

REFLECTION

DID YOU GET SOME OF YOUR GOALS ACCOMPLISHED TODAY?
_____
_____
_____
_____
_____
_____
_____
_____
_____

HEALTH CHECK

HOW MANY CUPS OF WATER DID YOU DRINK?

☐ YES ☐ NO

DID YOU EXERCISE TODAY?
(a 15-20 min. walk counts)

WHAT ARE YOU THE MOST PROUD OF TODAY?

WEDNESDAY

DATE : ____ ____ ____

WHAT'S ONE THING YOU'RE GRATEFUL FOR?
_____
_____
_____

LIST 3 MICRO GOALS YOU CAN TACKLE TODAY

1. _____
MICRO GOAL

2. _____
MICRO GOAL

3. _____
MICRO GOAL

BIG WINS / LESSONS

DAY 3

WHERE DO YOU SEE YOURSELF IN 5 YEARS?

NOTES / IDEAS

THURSDAY

DATE : ____ ____ ____

"Chaos isn't a pit. Chaos is a ladder." -Littlefinger, Character Game of Thrones

WHAT'S ONE THING YOU'RE GRATEFUL FOR?

_____
_____

LIST 3 MICRO GOALS YOU CAN TACKLE TODAY

1. _____
MICRO GOAL

2. _____
MICRO GOAL

3. _____
MICRO GOAL

BIG WINS / LESSONS

DAY 4

REFLECTION

DID YOU GET SOME OF YOUR GOALS ACCOMPLISHED TODAY?
_____
_____
_____
_____
_____
_____
_____
_____
_____

HEALTH CHECK

HOW MANY CUPS OF WATER DID YOU DRINK?

☐ YES ☐ NO

DID YOU EXERCISE TODAY?
(a 15-20 min. walk counts)

WHAT ARE YOU THE MOST PROUD OF TODAY?

FRIDAY

DATE : ____ ____ ____

WHAT'S ONE THING YOU'RE GRATEFUL FOR?

_____
_____
_____

> " If you don't think about the future, you won't have one. -Henry Ford "

LIST 3 MICRO GOALS YOU CAN TACKLE TODAY

1. _____
MICRO GOAL
_____
_____
_____
_____

2. _____
MICRO GOAL
_____
_____
_____
_____

3. _____
MICRO GOAL
_____
_____
_____
_____

BIG WINS / LESSONS

DAY 5

REFLECTION

DID YOU GET SOME OF YOUR GOALS ACCOMPLISHED TODAY?
_____
_____
_____
_____
_____
_____
_____
_____
_____

HEALTH CHECK

☐ ☐ ☐ ☐ ☐ ☐ ☐   HOW MANY CUPS OF WATER DID YOU DRINK?

☐   ☐   DID YOU EXERCISE TODAY?
YES   NO   (a 15-20 min. walk counts)

WHAT ARE YOU THE MOST PROUD OF TODAY?

SATURDAY

DATE : ____ ____ ____

WHAT'S ONE THING YOU'RE GRATEFUL FOR?

_____
_____
_____

LIST 3 MICRO GOALS YOU CAN TACKLE TODAY

1. _____
MICRO GOAL
_____
_____
_____
_____

2. _____
MICRO GOAL
_____
_____
_____
_____

3. _____
MICRO GOAL
_____
_____
_____
_____

BIG WINS / LESSONS

WHAT DID YOU GET ACCOMPLISHED THE PAST 5 DAYS?

WHAT ARE SOME THINGS YOU WANT TO DO DIFFERENTLY?

SUNDAY

DATE : ____ ____ ____

WHAT'S ONE THING YOU'RE GRATEFUL FOR?

_____
_____
_____
_____
_____

> " Ninety-nine percent of failure come from people who have a habit of making excuses. "

WHAT ARE 3 THINGS YOU CAN DO TODAY TO PREPARE FOR A SUCCESSFUL WEEK?

1. _____
   _____
   _____
   _____
   _____

2. _____
   _____
   _____
   _____
   _____

3. _____
   _____
   _____
   _____
   _____

WHAT IS SOMETHING YOU FEAR?

_____
_____
_____
_____
_____
_____
_____
_____
_____
_____
_____
_____
_____
_____
_____
_____
_____
_____
_____
_____

WHAT CAN WE DO TO CONQUER THIS?

MONDAY

DATE : ____ ____ ____

"A teacher affects eternity. He can never tell where his influence stops."
-Henry B. Adams, American historian

WHAT'S ONE THING YOU'RE GRATEFUL FOR?
_____
_____

LIST 3 MICRO GOALS YOU CAN TACKLE TODAY

1. _____
MICRO GOAL
_____
_____
_____
_____

2. _____
MICRO GOAL
_____
_____
_____
_____

3. _____
MICRO GOAL
_____
_____
_____
_____

BIG WINS / LESSONS

```
┌─────────────────────────────────────────────────────┐
│                                                     │
│                                                     │
│                                                     │
│                                                     │
│                                                     │
│                                                     │
└─────────────────────────────────────────────────────┘
```

DAY 8

REFLECTION

DID YOU GET SOME OF YOUR GOALS ACCOMPLISHED TODAY?
_____
_____
_____
_____
_____
_____
_____
_____
_____

HEALTH CHECK

HOW MANY CUPS OF WATER DID YOU DRINK?

☐ YES   ☐ NO

DID YOU EXERCISE TODAY?
(a 15-20 min. walk counts)

WHAT ARE YOU THE MOST PROUD OF TODAY?

TUESDAY

DATE : ____ ____ ____

WHAT'S ONE THING YOU'RE GRATEFUL FOR?

_____
_____
_____

> " **Action is eloquence.** *-Shakespeare* "

LIST 3 MICRO GOALS YOU CAN TACKLE TODAY

1. _____
MICRO GOAL
_____
_____
_____
_____

2. _____
MICRO GOAL
_____
_____
_____
_____

3. _____
MICRO GOAL
_____
_____
_____
_____

BIG WINS / LESSONS

DAY 9

REFLECTION

DID YOU GET SOME OF YOUR GOALS ACCOMPLISHED TODAY?

_____
_____
_____
_____
_____
_____
_____
_____

HEALTH CHECK

HOW MANY CUPS OF WATER DID YOU DRINK?

☐ YES ☐ NO

DID YOU EXERCISE TODAY?
(a 15-20 min. walk counts)

WHAT ARE YOU THE MOST PROUD OF TODAY?

WEDNESDAY

DATE : ____ ____ ___

WHAT'S ONE THING YOU'RE GRATEFUL FOR?
_____
_____
_____

LIST 3 MICRO GOALS YOU CAN TACKLE TODAY

1. _____
MICRO GOAL
_____
_____
_____
_____

2. _____
MICRO GOAL
_____
_____
_____
_____

3. _____
MICRO GOAL
_____
_____
_____
_____

BIG WINS / LESSONS

WHERE DO YOU SEE YOURSELF IN 1 YEAR?

NOTES / IDEAS

THURSDAY

DATE : ____ ____ ____

"Everyone lives by selling something." -Robert Louis Stevenson

WHAT'S ONE THING YOU'RE GRATEFUL FOR?

_____
_____
_____

LIST 3 MICRO GOALS YOU CAN TACKLE TODAY

1. _____
MICRO GOAL

_____
_____
_____
_____

2. _____
MICRO GOAL

_____
_____
_____
_____

3. _____
MICRO GOAL

_____
_____
_____
_____

BIG WINS / LESSONS

```
┌─────────────────────────────────────────┐
│                                         │
│                                         │
│                                         │
│                                         │
│                                         │
└─────────────────────────────────────────┘
```

DAY 11

REFLECTION

DID YOU GET SOME OF YOUR GOALS ACCOMPLISHED TODAY?
_____
_____
_____
_____
_____
_____
_____
_____
_____

HEALTH CHECK

HOW MANY CUPS OF WATER DID YOU DRINK?

☐ YES ☐ NO

DID YOU EXERCISE TODAY?
(a 15-20 min. walk counts)

WHAT ARE YOU THE MOST PROUD OF TODAY?

FRIDAY

DATE : ____ ____ ____

WHAT'S ONE THING YOU'RE GRATEFUL FOR?

___

> " In matters of style, swim with the current; in matters of principle, stand like a rock. "

LIST 3 MICRO GOALS YOU CAN TACKLE TODAY

1. _____
MICRO GOAL

2. _____
MICRO GOAL

3. _____
MICRO GOAL

BIG WINS / LESSONS

REFLECTION

DID YOU GET SOME OF YOUR GOALS ACCOMPLISHED TODAY?

_____
_____
_____
_____
_____
_____
_____
_____
_____

HEALTH CHECK

HOW MANY CUPS OF WATER DID YOU DRINK?

☐ YES ☐ NO

DID YOU EXERCISE TODAY?
(a 15-20 min. walk counts)

WHAT ARE YOU THE MOST PROUD OF TODAY?

SATURDAY

DATE : ____ ____ ___

WHAT'S ONE THING YOU'RE GRATEFUL FOR?
_____
_____
_____

LIST 3 MICRO GOALS YOU CAN TACKLE TODAY

1. _____
MICRO GOAL
_____
_____
_____
_____

2. _____
MICRO GOAL
_____
_____
_____
_____

3. _____
MICRO GOAL
_____
_____
_____
_____

BIG WINS / LESSONS

DAY 13

WHAT DID YOU GET ACCOMPLISHED THE PAST 5 DAYS?

WHAT ARE SOME THINGS YOU WANT TO DO DIFFERENTLY?

SUNDAY

DATE : ____ ____ ____

WHAT'S ONE THING YOU'RE GRATEFUL FOR?

_____
_____
_____
_____

> "A leader is a dealer in hope." —Napoleon Bonaparte

WHAT ARE 3 THINGS YOU CAN DO TODAY TO PREPARE FOR A SUCCESSFUL WEEK?

1. _____
_____
_____
_____
_____

2. _____
_____
_____
_____
_____

3. _____
_____
_____
_____
_____

WHAT DID YOU GET ACCOMPLISHED THE PAST 5 DAYS?

WHAT ARE SOME THINGS YOU WANT TO DO DIFFERENTLY?

MONDAY

DATE : ____ ____ ____

"Patience and perseverance have a magical effect before which difficulties disappear and obstacles vanish." -John Quincy Adams

WHAT'S ONE THING YOU'RE GRATEFUL FOR?

_____
_____
_____

LIST 3 MICRO GOALS YOU CAN TACKLE TODAY

1. _____
MICRO GOAL

_____
_____
_____
_____

2. _____
MICRO GOAL

_____
_____
_____
_____

3. _____
MICRO GOAL

_____
_____
_____
_____

BIG WINS / LESSONS

DAY 15

REFLECTION

DID YOU GET SOME OF YOUR GOALS ACCOMPLISHED TODAY?
_____
_____
_____
_____
_____
_____
_____
_____

HEALTH CHECK

HOW MANY CUPS OF WATER DID YOU DRINK?

☐ YES ☐ NO

DID YOU EXERCISE TODAY?
(a 15-20 min. walk counts)

WHAT ARE YOU THE MOST PROUD OF TODAY?

TUESDAY

DATE : _____ _____ _____

WHAT'S ONE THING YOU'RE GRATEFUL FOR?
___
___
___

> "He who has a why can endure any how." —*Friedrich Nietzsche*

LIST 3 MICRO GOALS YOU CAN TACKLE TODAY

1. ___
MICRO GOAL
___
___
___
___

2. ___
MICRO GOAL
___
___
___
___

3. ___
MICRO GOAL
___
___
___
___

BIG WINS / LESSONS

DAY 16

REFLECTION

DID YOU GET SOME OF YOUR GOALS ACCOMPLISHED TODAY?

_____
_____
_____
_____
_____
_____
_____
_____
_____

HEALTH CHECK

☐ ☐ ☐ ☐ ☐ ☐ ☐ HOW MANY CUPS OF WATER DID YOU DRINK?

☐ YES ☐ NO DID YOU EXERCISE TODAY?
(a 15-20 min. walk counts)

WHAT ARE YOU THE MOST PROUD OF TODAY?

WEDNESDAY

DATE : ____ ____ ____

WHAT'S ONE THING YOU'RE GRATEFUL FOR?
_____
_____
_____

LIST 3 MICRO GOALS YOU CAN TACKLE TODAY

1. _____
MICRO GOAL
_____
_____
_____
_____

2. _____
MICRO GOAL
_____
_____
_____
_____

3. _____
MICRO GOAL
_____
_____
_____
_____

BIG WINS / LESSONS

DAY 17

NOTES / IDEAS

THURSDAY

DATE : ____ ____ ____

"Nothing so conclusively proves a man's ability to lead others as what he does from day to day to lead himself."
—Thomas J. Watson
Former CEO, IBM

WHAT'S ONE THING YOU'RE GRATEFUL FOR?

_____
_____

LIST 3 MICRO GOALS YOU CAN TACKLE TODAY

1. _____
MICRO GOAL

_____
_____
_____
_____

2. _____
MICRO GOAL

_____
_____
_____
_____

3. _____
MICRO GOAL

_____
_____
_____
_____

BIG WINS / LESSONS

DAY 18

REFLECTION

DID YOU GET SOME OF YOUR GOALS ACCOMPLISHED TODAY?
_____
_____
_____
_____
_____
_____
_____
_____

HEALTH CHECK

HOW MANY CUPS OF WATER DID YOU DRINK?

☐ YES   ☐ NO

DID YOU EXERCISE TODAY?
(a 15-20 min. walk counts)

WHAT ARE YOU THE MOST PROUD OF TODAY?

FRIDAY

DATE : ____ ____ ____

WHAT'S ONE THING YOU'RE GRATEFUL FOR?
_____
_____

> " *A mediocre idea that generates enthusiasm will go further than a great idea that inspires no one.* " -Mary Kay Ash

LIST 3 MICRO GOALS YOU CAN TACKLE TODAY

1. _____
MICRO GOAL
_____
_____
_____
_____

2. _____
MICRO GOAL
_____
_____
_____
_____

3. _____
MICRO GOAL
_____
_____
_____
_____

BIG WINS / LESSONS

```
┌──────────────────────────────────────────────┐
│                                              │
│                                              │
│                                              │
│                                              │
└──────────────────────────────────────────────┘
```

DAY 19

REFLECTION

DID YOU GET SOME OF YOUR GOALS ACCOMPLISHED TODAY?
___
___
___
___
___
___
___
___
___

HEALTH CHECK

HOW MANY CUPS OF WATER DID YOU DRINK?

☐ YES ☐ NO

DID YOU EXERCISE TODAY?
(a 15-20 min. walk counts)

WHAT ARE YOU THE MOST PROUD OF TODAY?

SATURDAY

DATE : ____ ____ ____

WHAT'S ONE THING YOU'RE GRATEFUL FOR?

_____
_____
_____

LIST 3 MICRO GOALS YOU CAN TACKLE TODAY

1. _____
MICRO GOAL

_____
_____
_____
_____

2. _____
MICRO GOAL

_____
_____
_____
_____

3. _____
MICRO GOAL

_____
_____
_____
_____

BIG WINS / LESSONS

DAY 20

WHAT DID YOU GET ACCOMPLISHED THE PAST 5 DAYS?

WHAT ARE SOME THINGS YOU WANT TO DO DIFFERENTLY?

SUNDAY

DATE : ____ ____ ____

WHAT'S ONE THING YOU'RE GRATEFUL FOR?

_____
_____
_____
_____

> "Life is a challenge, meet it." —Mother Theresa

WHAT ARE 3 THINGS YOU CAN DO TODAY TO PREPARE FOR A SUCCESSFUL WEEK?

1. _____
_____
_____
_____
_____

2. _____
_____
_____
_____
_____

3. _____
_____
_____
_____
_____

WHAT DID YOU GET ACCOMPLISHED THE PAST 5 DAYS?

WHAT ARE SOME THINGS YOU WANT TO DO DIFFERENTLY?

MONDAY

DATE : ____ ____ ____

"Leadership is the art of getting someone else to do something you want done because he wants to do it." -Dwight D. Eisenhower

WHAT'S ONE THING YOU'RE GRATEFUL FOR?

_____
_____

LIST 3 MICRO GOALS YOU CAN TACKLE TODAY

1. _____
MICRO GOAL
_____
_____
_____
_____

2. _____
MICRO GOAL
_____
_____
_____
_____

3. _____
MICRO GOAL
_____
_____
_____
_____

BIG WINS / LESSONS

DAY 22

REFLECTION

DID YOU GET SOME OF YOUR GOALS ACCOMPLISHED TODAY?
_____
_____
_____
_____
_____
_____
_____
_____
_____

HEALTH CHECK

HOW MANY CUPS OF WATER DID YOU DRINK?

☐ YES ☐ NO

DID YOU EXERCISE TODAY?
(a 15-20 min. walk counts)

WHAT ARE YOU THE MOST PROUD OF TODAY?

TUESDAY

DATE : ___ ___ ___

WHAT'S ONE THING YOU'RE GRATEFUL FOR?

_____
_____
_____

> "Two things are bad for the heart—running uphill and running down people."
> -Bernard Gimbel

LIST 3 MICRO GOALS YOU CAN TACKLE TODAY

1. _____
MICRO GOAL
_____
_____
_____
_____

2. _____
MICRO GOAL
_____
_____
_____
_____

3. _____
MICRO GOAL
_____
_____
_____
_____

BIG WINS / LESSONS

DAY 23

REFLECTION

DID YOU GET SOME OF YOUR GOALS ACCOMPLISHED TODAY?
_____
_____
_____
_____
_____
_____
_____
_____
_____

HEALTH CHECK

HOW MANY CUPS OF WATER DID YOU DRINK?

☐ YES ☐ NO

DID YOU EXERCISE TODAY?
(a 15-20 min. walk counts)

WHAT ARE YOU THE MOST PROUD OF TODAY?

WEDNESDAY

DATE : ____ ____ ____

WHAT'S ONE THING YOU'RE GRATEFUL FOR?
_____
_____
_____

LIST 3 MICRO GOALS YOU CAN TACKLE TODAY

1. _____
MICRO GOAL
_____
_____
_____
_____

2. _____
MICRO GOAL
_____
_____
_____
_____

3. _____
MICRO GOAL
_____
_____
_____
_____

BIG WINS / LESSONS

```
┌─────────────────────────────────────────┐
│                                         │
│                                         │
│                                         │
│                                         │
│                                         │
└─────────────────────────────────────────┘
```

DAY 24

NOTES / IDEAS

THURSDAY

DATE : ____ ____ ____

"Nothing so conclusively proves a man's ability to lead others as what he does from day to day to lead himself." -Thomas J. Watson
Former CEO, IBM

WHAT'S ONE THING YOU'RE GRATEFUL FOR?

___

LIST 3 MICRO GOALS YOU CAN TACKLE TODAY

1. _____
MICRO GOAL

2. _____
MICRO GOAL

3. _____
MICRO GOAL

BIG WINS / LESSONS

DAY 25

REFLECTION

DID YOU GET SOME OF YOUR GOALS ACCOMPLISHED TODAY?
_____
_____
_____
_____
_____
_____
_____
_____
_____

HEALTH CHECK

☐ ☐ ☐ ☐ ☐ ☐ ☐   HOW MANY CUPS OF WATER DID YOU DRINK?

☐ YES   ☐ NO   DID YOU EXERCISE TODAY?
(a 15-20 min. walk counts)

WHAT ARE YOU THE MOST PROUD OF TODAY?

FRIDAY

DATE : ____ ____ ____

WHAT'S ONE THING YOU'RE GRATEFUL FOR?

_____
_____
_____

> " A mediocre idea that generates enthusiasm will go further than a great idea that inspires no one. " *-Mary Kay Ash*

LIST 3 MICRO GOALS YOU CAN TACKLE TODAY

1. _____
MICRO GOAL
_____
_____
_____
_____

2. _____
MICRO GOAL
_____
_____
_____
_____

3. _____
MICRO GOAL
_____
_____
_____
_____

BIG WINS / LESSONS

DAY 26

REFLECTION

DID YOU GET SOME OF YOUR GOALS ACCOMPLISHED TODAY?
_____
_____
_____
_____
_____
_____
_____
_____
_____

HEALTH CHECK

☐ ☐ ☐ ☐ ☐ ☐ ☐   HOW MANY CUPS OF WATER DID YOU DRINK?

☐ YES ☐ NO   DID YOU EXERCISE TODAY?
(a 15-20 min. walk counts)

WHAT ARE YOU THE MOST PROUD OF TODAY?

SATURDAY

DATE : ____ ____ ____

WHAT'S ONE THING YOU'RE GRATEFUL FOR?
_____
_____
_____

LIST 3 MICRO GOALS YOU CAN TACKLE TODAY

1. _____
MICRO GOAL
_____
_____
_____
_____

2. _____
MICRO GOAL
_____
_____
_____
_____

3. _____
MICRO GOAL
_____
_____
_____
_____

BIG WINS / LESSONS

WHAT DID YOU GET ACCOMPLISHED THE PAST 5 DAYS?

WHAT ARE SOME THINGS YOU WANT TO DO DIFFERENTLY?

SUNDAY

DATE : ____ ____ ____

WHAT'S ONE THING YOU'RE GRATEFUL FOR?

___

> **"** Life is a challenge, meet it. **"** —Mother Theresa

WHAT ARE 3 THINGS YOU CAN DO TODAY TO PREPARE FOR A SUCCESSFUL WEEK?

1. _____

2. _____

3. _____

WHAT DID YOU GET ACCOMPLISHED THE PAST 5 DAYS?

WHAT ARE SOME THINGS YOU WANT TO DO DIFFERENTLY?

MONDAY

DATE : ____ ____ ____

"Shallow people believe in luck. Wise and strong people believe in cause and effect." -Waldo Emerson

WHAT'S ONE THING YOU'RE GRATEFUL FOR?

LIST 3 MICRO GOALS YOU CAN TACKLE TODAY

1. _____
MICRO GOAL

2. _____
MICRO GOAL

3. _____
MICRO GOAL

BIG WINS / LESSONS

DAY 29

REFLECTION

DID YOU GET SOME OF YOUR GOALS ACCOMPLISHED TODAY?
_____
_____
_____
_____
_____
_____
_____
_____

HEALTH CHECK

HOW MANY CUPS OF WATER DID YOU DRINK?

☐ YES ☐ NO

DID YOU EXERCISE TODAY?
(a 15-20 min. walk counts)

WHAT ARE YOU THE MOST PROUD OF TODAY?

TUESDAY

DATE : ____ ____ ____

WHAT'S ONE THING YOU'RE GRATEFUL FOR?

___

> " Discipline is remembering what you want. "
>
> *-David Campbell, founder Saks Fifth Avenue*

LIST 3 MICRO GOALS YOU CAN TACKLE TODAY

1. _____
MICRO GOAL

2. _____
MICRO GOAL

3. _____
MICRO GOAL

BIG WINS / LESSONS

DAY 30

REFLECTION

DID YOU GET SOME OF YOUR GOALS ACCOMPLISHED TODAY?
___
___
___
___
___
___
___
___

HEALTH CHECK

HOW MANY CUPS OF WATER DID YOU DRINK?

☐ YES   ☐ NO

DID YOU EXERCISE TODAY?
(a 15-20 min. walk counts)

WHAT ARE YOU THE MOST PROUD OF TODAY?

WEDNESDAY

DATE : ____ ____ ___

WHAT'S ONE THING YOU'RE GRATEFUL FOR?
_____
_____
_____

LIST 3 MICRO GOALS YOU CAN TACKLE TODAY

1. _____
MICRO GOAL

2. _____
MICRO GOAL

3. _____
MICRO GOAL

BIG WINS / LESSONS

DAY 31

NOTES / IDEAS

THURSDAY

DATE : _____ _____ _____

"I not only use all the brains I have, but all I can borrow."
-Woodrow Wilson

WHAT'S ONE THING YOU'RE GRATEFUL FOR?

_____
_____

LIST 3 MICRO GOALS YOU CAN TACKLE TODAY

1. _____
MICRO GOAL

_____
_____
_____
_____

2. _____
MICRO GOAL

_____
_____
_____
_____

3. _____
MICRO GOAL

_____
_____
_____
_____

BIG WINS / LESSONS

DAY 32

REFLECTION

DID YOU GET SOME OF YOUR GOALS ACCOMPLISHED TODAY?

_____
_____
_____
_____
_____
_____
_____
_____
_____

HEALTH CHECK

HOW MANY CUPS OF WATER DID YOU DRINK?

☐ YES ☐ NO

DID YOU EXERCISE TODAY?
(a 15-20 min. walk counts)

WHAT ARE YOU THE MOST PROUD OF TODAY?

FRIDAY

DATE : ____ ____ ____

WHAT'S ONE THING YOU'RE GRATEFUL FOR?
___

> "Every organization must be prepared to abandon everything it does to survive in the future." *-Peter Drucker*

LIST 3 MICRO GOALS YOU CAN TACKLE TODAY

1. _____
MICRO GOAL
___

2. _____
MICRO GOAL
___

3. _____
MICRO GOAL
___

BIG WINS / LESSONS

DAY 33

REFLECTION

DID YOU GET SOME OF YOUR GOALS ACCOMPLISHED TODAY?

_____
_____
_____
_____
_____
_____
_____
_____

HEALTH CHECK

HOW MANY CUPS OF WATER DID YOU DRINK?

☐ YES ☐ NO

DID YOU EXERCISE TODAY?
(a 15-20 min. walk counts)

WHAT ARE YOU THE MOST PROUD OF TODAY?

SATURDAY

DATE : ____ ____ ____

WHAT'S ONE THING YOU'RE GRATEFUL FOR?
_____
_____
_____

LIST 3 MICRO GOALS YOU CAN TACKLE TODAY

1. _____
MICRO GOAL

2. _____
MICRO GOAL

3. _____
MICRO GOAL

BIG WINS / LESSONS

DAY 34

WHAT DID YOU GET ACCOMPLISHED THE PAST 5 DAYS?

WHAT ARE SOME THINGS YOU WANT TO DO DIFFERENTLY?

SUNDAY

DATE : ____ ____ ____

WHAT'S ONE THING YOU'RE GRATEFUL FOR?

_____
_____
_____
_____
_____

> "You can't change people. You must be the change you wish to see in people." -Gandhi

WHAT ARE 3 THINGS YOU CAN DO TODAY TO PREPARE FOR A SUCCESSFUL WEEK?

1. _____
_____
_____
_____
_____

2. _____
_____
_____
_____
_____

3. _____
_____
_____
_____
_____

WHAT DID YOU GET ACCOMPLISHED THE PAST 5 DAYS?

WHAT ARE SOME THINGS YOU WANT TO DO DIFFERENTLY?

MONDAY

DATE : ____ ____ ____

"There is no such thing as constructive criticism." -Dale Carnegie

WHAT'S ONE THING YOU'RE GRATEFUL FOR?

_____
_____

LIST 3 MICRO GOALS YOU CAN TACKLE TODAY

1. _____
MICRO GOAL

2. _____
MICRO GOAL

3. _____
MICRO GOAL

BIG WINS / LESSONS

DAY 36

REFLECTION

DID YOU GET SOME OF YOUR GOALS ACCOMPLISHED TODAY?
_____
_____
_____
_____
_____
_____
_____
_____
_____

HEALTH CHECK

☐ ☐ ☐ ☐ ☐ ☐ ☐   HOW MANY CUPS OF WATER DID YOU DRINK?

☐ YES ☐ NO   DID YOU EXERCISE TODAY?
(a 15-20 min. walk counts)

WHAT ARE YOU THE MOST PROUD OF TODAY?

TUESDAY

DATE : ____ ____ ___

WHAT'S ONE THING YOU'RE GRATEFUL FOR?

> *"Unless commitment is made, there are only promises and hopes... but no plans."* — Peter Drucker

LIST 3 MICRO GOALS YOU CAN TACKLE TODAY

1. _____
MICRO GOAL

2. _____
MICRO GOAL

3. _____
MICRO GOAL

BIG WINS / LESSONS

DAY 37

REFLECTION

DID YOU GET SOME OF YOUR GOALS ACCOMPLISHED TODAY?
_____
_____
_____
_____
_____
_____
_____
_____
_____

HEALTH CHECK

HOW MANY CUPS OF WATER DID YOU DRINK?

☐ YES   ☐ NO

DID YOU EXERCISE TODAY?
(a 15-20 min. walk counts)

WHAT ARE YOU THE MOST PROUD OF TODAY?

WEDNESDAY

DATE : ____ ____ ____

WHAT'S ONE THING YOU'RE GRATEFUL FOR?
_____
_____
_____

LIST 3 MICRO GOALS YOU CAN TACKLE TODAY

1. _____
MICRO GOAL
_____
_____
_____
_____

2. _____
MICRO GOAL
_____
_____
_____
_____

3. _____
MICRO GOAL
_____
_____
_____
_____

BIG WINS / LESSONS

NOTES / IDEAS

THURSDAY

DATE : ____ ____ ____

"Although some people think that life is a battle, it is actually a game of giving and receiving." -Florence Scovill Shinn, philosopher and author

WHAT'S ONE THING YOU'RE GRATEFUL FOR?

_____
_____

LIST 3 MICRO GOALS YOU CAN TACKLE TODAY

1. _____
MICRO GOAL

2. _____
MICRO GOAL

3. _____
MICRO GOAL

BIG WINS / LESSONS

REFLECTION

DID YOU GET SOME OF YOUR GOALS ACCOMPLISHED TODAY?
_____
_____
_____
_____
_____
_____
_____
_____

HEALTH CHECK

HOW MANY CUPS OF WATER DID YOU DRINK?

☐ YES ☐ NO

DID YOU EXERCISE TODAY?
(a 15-20 min. walk counts)

WHAT ARE YOU THE MOST PROUD OF TODAY?

FRIDAY

DATE : ____ ____ ____

WHAT'S ONE THING YOU'RE GRATEFUL FOR?
_____
_____
_____

> " *Leaders don't create followers, they create more leaders.* " —*Tom Peters*

LIST 3 MICRO GOALS YOU CAN TACKLE TODAY

1. _____
MICRO GOAL
_____
_____
_____
_____

2. _____
MICRO GOAL
_____
_____
_____
_____

3. _____
MICRO GOAL
_____
_____
_____
_____

BIG WINS / LESSONS

DAY 40

REFLECTION

DID YOU GET SOME OF YOUR GOALS ACCOMPLISHED TODAY?
_____
_____
_____
_____
_____
_____
_____
_____
_____

HEALTH CHECK

▽ ▽ ▽ ▽ ▽ ▽ ▽ ▽   HOW MANY CUPS OF WATER DID YOU DRINK?

☐   ☐   DID YOU EXERCISE TODAY?
YES   NO   (a 15-20 min. walk counts)

WHAT ARE YOU THE MOST PROUD OF TODAY?

SATURDAY

DATE : ____ ____ ____

WHAT'S ONE THING YOU'RE GRATEFUL FOR?

LIST 3 MICRO GOALS YOU CAN TACKLE TODAY

1. _____
MICRO GOAL

---

2. _____
MICRO GOAL

---

3. _____
MICRO GOAL

BIG WINS / LESSONS

DAY 41

WHAT DID YOU GET ACCOMPLISHED THE PAST 5 DAYS?

_____
_____
_____
_____
_____
_____
_____
_____
_____
_____
_____
_____
_____
_____
_____

WHAT ARE SOME THINGS YOU WANT TO DO DIFFERENTLY?

_____
_____
_____
_____
_____
_____
_____
_____
_____
_____
_____
_____
_____
_____
_____
_____
_____
_____

SUNDAY

DATE : ____ ____ ____

WHAT'S ONE THING YOU'RE GRATEFUL FOR?

___

> " I never gave them hell. I just tell the truth and they think it's hell. "
> -Harry Truman

WHAT ARE 3 THINGS YOU CAN DO TODAY TO PREPARE FOR A SUCCESSFUL WEEK?

1. _____

2. _____

3. _____

DAY 42

WHAT DID YOU GET ACCOMPLISHED THE PAST 5 DAYS?

WHAT ARE SOME THINGS YOU WANT TO DO DIFFERENTLY?

MONDAY

DATE : ____ ____ ____

" The best way out is always through." -Robert Frost

WHAT'S ONE THING YOU'RE GRATEFUL FOR?
_____
_____

LIST 3 MICRO GOALS YOU CAN TACKLE TODAY

1. _____
MICRO GOAL
_____
_____
_____
_____

2. _____
MICRO GOAL
_____
_____
_____
_____

3. _____
MICRO GOAL
_____
_____
_____
_____

BIG WINS / LESSONS

DAY 43

REFLECTION

DID YOU GET SOME OF YOUR GOALS ACCOMPLISHED TODAY?
_____
_____
_____
_____
_____
_____
_____
_____
_____

HEALTH CHECK

HOW MANY CUPS OF WATER DID YOU DRINK?

☐ YES ☐ NO

DID YOU EXERCISE TODAY?
(a 15-20 min. walk counts)

WHAT ARE YOU THE MOST PROUD OF TODAY?

TUESDAY

DATE : ___ ___ ___

WHAT'S ONE THING YOU'RE GRATEFUL FOR?

___

> " *Performance is your reality. Forget everything else.* " — *Harold Geneen, CEO, ITT*

LIST 3 MICRO GOALS YOU CAN TACKLE TODAY

1. _____
MICRO GOAL

2. _____
MICRO GOAL

3. _____
MICRO GOAL

BIG WINS / LESSONS

DAY 44

REFLECTION

DID YOU GET SOME OF YOUR GOALS ACCOMPLISHED TODAY?
_____
_____
_____
_____
_____
_____
_____
_____
_____

HEALTH CHECK

HOW MANY CUPS OF WATER DID YOU DRINK?

☐ YES ☐ NO

DID YOU EXERCISE TODAY?
(a 15-20 min. walk counts)

WHAT ARE YOU THE MOST PROUD OF TODAY?

WEDNESDAY

DATE : _____ _____ _____

WHAT'S ONE THING YOU'RE GRATEFUL FOR?
_____
_____
_____

LIST 3 MICRO GOALS YOU CAN TACKLE TODAY

1. _____
MICRO GOAL
   _____
   _____
   _____
   _____

2. _____
MICRO GOAL
   _____
   _____
   _____
   _____

3. _____
MICRO GOAL
   _____
   _____
   _____
   _____

BIG WINS / LESSONS

```
┌─────────────────────────────────────────┐
│                                         │
│                                         │
│                                         │
│                                         │
│                                         │
└─────────────────────────────────────────┘
```

DAY 45

NOTES / IDEAS

THURSDAY

DATE : ____ ____ ____

"There is only one boss: the customer." -Sam Walton

WHAT'S ONE THING YOU'RE GRATEFUL FOR?
_____
_____
_____

LIST 3 MICRO GOALS YOU CAN TACKLE TODAY

1. _____
MICRO GOAL
_____
_____
_____
_____

2. _____
MICRO GOAL
_____
_____
_____
_____

3. _____
MICRO GOAL
_____
_____
_____
_____

BIG WINS / LESSONS

```
┌─────────────────────────────────────────┐
│                                         │
│                                         │
│                                         │
│                                         │
│                                         │
│                                         │
└─────────────────────────────────────────┘
```

DAY 46

REFLECTION

DID YOU GET SOME OF YOUR GOALS ACCOMPLISHED TODAY?

_____
_____
_____
_____
_____
_____
_____
_____
_____

HEALTH CHECK

HOW MANY CUPS OF WATER DID YOU DRINK?

☐ YES ☐ NO

DID YOU EXERCISE TODAY?
(a 15-20 min. walk counts)

WHAT ARE YOU THE MOST PROUD OF TODAY?

FRIDAY

DATE : ___ ___ ___

WHAT'S ONE THING YOU'RE GRATEFUL FOR?

___

> " Show me a man who cannot bother to do little things and I'll show you a man who cannot be trusted to do big things. "
> -Lawrence D. Bell, founder, Bell Aircraft

LIST 3 MICRO GOALS YOU CAN TACKLE TODAY

1. _____
MICRO GOAL

2. _____
MICRO GOAL

3. _____
MICRO GOAL

BIG WINS / LESSONS

DAY 47

REFLECTION

DID YOU GET SOME OF YOUR GOALS ACCOMPLISHED TODAY?
_____
_____
_____
_____
_____
_____
_____
_____
_____

HEALTH CHECK

☐ ☐ ☐ ☐ ☐ ☐ ☐   HOW MANY CUPS OF WATER DID YOU DRINK?

☐ YES ☐ NO   DID YOU EXERCISE TODAY?
(a 15-20 min. walk counts)

WHAT ARE YOU THE MOST PROUD OF TODAY?

SATURDAY

DATE : ____ ____ ____

WHAT'S ONE THING YOU'RE GRATEFUL FOR?
_____
_____
_____

LIST 3 MICRO GOALS YOU CAN TACKLE TODAY

1. _____

MICRO GOAL

_____
_____
_____
_____

2. _____

MICRO GOAL

_____
_____
_____
_____

3. _____

MICRO GOAL

_____
_____
_____
_____

BIG WINS / LESSONS

WHAT DID YOU GET ACCOMPLISHED THE PAST 5 DAYS?

WHAT ARE SOME THINGS YOU WANT TO DO DIFFERENTLY?

SUNDAY

DATE : ____ ____ ____

WHAT'S ONE THING YOU'RE GRATEFUL FOR?

_____
_____
_____
_____
_____

> ❝ Man must not allow the clock and the calendar to bind him to the fact that each moment of him to the fact that each moment of his life is miracle and a mystery. ❞
> -H.G. Wells

WHAT ARE 3 THINGS YOU CAN DO TODAY TO PREPARE FOR A SUCCESSFUL WEEK?

1. _____

2. _____

3. _____

WHAT DID YOU GET ACCOMPLISHED THE PAST 5 DAYS?

WHAT ARE SOME THINGS YOU WANT TO DO DIFFERENTLY?

MONDAY

DATE : ____ ____ ____

" Discipline is the bridge between goals and accomplishments."
-Jim Rohn, author and motivator

WHAT'S ONE THING YOU'RE GRATEFUL FOR?
_____
_____
_____

LIST 3 MICRO GOALS YOU CAN TACKLE TODAY

1. _____
MICRO GOAL
_____
_____
_____
_____

2. _____
MICRO GOAL
_____
_____
_____
_____

3. _____
MICRO GOAL
_____
_____
_____
_____

BIG WINS / LESSONS

REFLECTION

DID YOU GET SOME OF YOUR GOALS ACCOMPLISHED TODAY?
_____
_____
_____
_____
_____
_____
_____
_____
_____

HEALTH CHECK

HOW MANY CUPS OF WATER DID YOU DRINK?

☐ YES ☐ NO

DID YOU EXERCISE TODAY?
(a 15-20 min. walk counts)

WHAT ARE YOU THE MOST PROUD OF TODAY?

TUESDAY

DATE : ____ ____ ____

WHAT'S ONE THING YOU'RE GRATEFUL FOR?

___

> " We make a living by what we get, but we make a life by what we give.
> - *Harold Geneen, CEO, ITT* "

LIST 3 MICRO GOALS YOU CAN TACKLE TODAY

1. _____
MICRO GOAL

2. _____
MICRO GOAL

3. _____
MICRO GOAL

BIG WINS / LESSONS

REFLECTION

DID YOU GET SOME OF YOUR GOALS ACCOMPLISHED TODAY?
_____
_____
_____
_____
_____
_____
_____
_____
_____

HEALTH CHECK

HOW MANY CUPS OF WATER DID YOU DRINK?

☐ YES   ☐ NO

DID YOU EXERCISE TODAY?
(a 15-20 min. walk counts)

WHAT ARE YOU THE MOST PROUD OF TODAY?

WEDNESDAY

DATE : ____ ____ ____

WHAT'S ONE THING YOU'RE GRATEFUL FOR?
_____
_____
_____

LIST 3 MICRO GOALS YOU CAN TACKLE TODAY

1. _____
MICRO GOAL
_____
_____
_____
_____

2. _____
MICRO GOAL
_____
_____
_____
_____

3. _____
MICRO GOAL
_____
_____
_____
_____

BIG WINS / LESSONS

DAY 52

NOTES / IDEAS

THURSDAY

DATE : ____ ____ ____

" A frightened captain makes a frightened crew."
-Lister Sinclair, playwright and broadcaster

WHAT'S ONE THING YOU'RE GRATEFUL FOR?
_____
_____

LIST 3 MICRO GOALS YOU CAN TACKLE TODAY

1. _____
MICRO GOAL

2. _____
MICRO GOAL

3. _____
MICRO GOAL

BIG WINS / LESSONS

DAY 53

REFLECTION

DID YOU GET SOME OF YOUR GOALS ACCOMPLISHED TODAY?
_____
_____
_____
_____
_____
_____
_____
_____
_____

HEALTH CHECK

HOW MANY CUPS OF WATER DID YOU DRINK?

☐ YES ☐ NO

DID YOU EXERCISE TODAY?
(a 15-20 min. walk counts)

WHAT ARE YOU THE MOST PROUD OF TODAY?

FRIDAY

DATE : ___ ___ ___

WHAT'S ONE THING YOU'RE GRATEFUL FOR?

___
___
___

> ❝ I want to be in the arena. I want to be brave with my life. And when we make the choice to dare greatly, we sign up to get our asses kicked. We can choose courage or we can choose comfort, but we can't have both. Not at the same time. ❞ *-Brené Brown*

LIST 3 MICRO GOALS YOU CAN TACKLE TODAY

1. _____
MICRO GOAL

2. _____
MICRO GOAL

3. _____
MICRO GOAL

BIG WINS / LESSONS

DAY 54

REFLECTION

DID YOU GET SOME OF YOUR GOALS ACCOMPLISHED TODAY?
_____
_____
_____
_____
_____
_____
_____
_____

HEALTH CHECK

☐ ☐ ☐ ☐ ☐ ☐ ☐ ☐   HOW MANY CUPS OF WATER DID YOU DRINK?

☐ YES   ☐ NO   DID YOU EXERCISE TODAY?
(a 15-20 min. walk counts)

WHAT ARE YOU THE MOST PROUD OF TODAY?

SATURDAY

DATE : ____ ____ ____

WHAT'S ONE THING YOU'RE GRATEFUL FOR?

_____
_____
_____

LIST 3 MICRO GOALS YOU CAN TACKLE TODAY

1. _____
MICRO GOAL
_____
_____
_____
_____

2. _____
MICRO GOAL
_____
_____
_____
_____

3. _____
MICRO GOAL
_____
_____
_____
_____

BIG WINS / LESSONS

WHAT DID YOU GET ACCOMPLISHED THE PAST 5 DAYS?

WHAT ARE SOME THINGS YOU WANT TO DO DIFFERENTLY?

SUNDAY

DATE : ____ ____ ____

WHAT'S ONE THING YOU'RE GRATEFUL FOR?

_____
_____
_____
_____

> "We forget: In life, it doesn't matter what happens to you or where you came from. It matters what you do with what happens and what you've been given."
> -Ryan Holiday, The Obstacle Is the Way

WHAT ARE 3 THINGS YOU CAN DO TODAY TO PREPARE FOR A SUCCESSFUL WEEK?

1. _____

2. _____

3. _____

WHAT DID YOU GET ACCOMPLISHED THE PAST 5 DAYS?

WHAT ARE SOME THINGS YOU WANT TO DO DIFFERENTLY?

MONDAY

DATE : _____ _____ _____

"Don't just sit there. Do something. The answers will follow."
-Mark Manson

WHAT'S ONE THING YOU'RE GRATEFUL FOR?
_____
_____

LIST 3 MICRO GOALS YOU CAN TACKLE TODAY

1. _____
MICRO GOAL
_____
_____
_____
_____

2. _____
MICRO GOAL
_____
_____
_____
_____

3. _____
MICRO GOAL
_____
_____
_____
_____

BIG WINS / LESSONS

DAY 57

REFLECTION

DID YOU GET SOME OF YOUR GOALS ACCOMPLISHED TODAY?

_____
_____
_____
_____
_____
_____
_____
_____
_____

HEALTH CHECK

HOW MANY CUPS OF WATER DID YOU DRINK?

☐ YES ☐ NO

DID YOU EXERCISE TODAY?
(a 15-20 min. walk counts)

WHAT ARE YOU THE MOST PROUD OF TODAY?

TUESDAY

DATE : ____ ____ ____

WHAT'S ONE THING YOU'RE GRATEFUL FOR?
_____
_____
_____

> " If you don't pay appropriate attention to what has your attention, it will take more of your attention than it deserves. " *- Harold Geneen, CEO, ITT*

LIST 3 MICRO GOALS YOU CAN TACKLE TODAY

1. _____
MICRO GOAL
_____
_____
_____
_____

2. _____
MICRO GOAL
_____
_____
_____
_____

3. _____
MICRO GOAL
_____
_____
_____
_____

BIG WINS / LESSONS

DAY 58

REFLECTION

DID YOU GET SOME OF YOUR GOALS ACCOMPLISHED TODAY?
_____
_____
_____
_____
_____
_____
_____
_____
_____

HEALTH CHECK

☐ ☐ ☐ ☐ ☐ ☐ ☐   HOW MANY CUPS OF WATER DID YOU DRINK?

☐ ☐   DID YOU EXERCISE TODAY?
YES NO   (a 15-20 min. walk counts)

WHAT ARE YOU THE MOST PROUD OF TODAY?

WEDNESDAY

DATE : ____ ____ ____

WHAT'S ONE THING YOU'RE GRATEFUL FOR?

_____
_____
_____

LIST 3 MICRO GOALS YOU CAN TACKLE TODAY

1. _____
MICRO GOAL

_____
_____
_____
_____

2. _____
MICRO GOAL

_____
_____
_____
_____

3. _____
MICRO GOAL

_____
_____
_____
_____

BIG WINS / LESSONS

+--+
| |
| |
| |
| |
+--+

DAY 59

NOTES / IDEAS

THURSDAY

DATE : ____ ____ ____

"In every situation, life is asking us a question, and our actions are the answer."
-Ryan Holiday

WHAT'S ONE THING YOU'RE GRATEFUL FOR?

_____
_____

LIST 3 MICRO GOALS YOU CAN TACKLE TODAY

1. _____
MICRO GOAL

_____
_____
_____
_____

2. _____
MICRO GOAL

_____
_____
_____
_____

3. _____
MICRO GOAL

_____
_____
_____
_____

BIG WINS / LESSONS

DAY 60

REFLECTION

DID YOU GET SOME OF YOUR GOALS ACCOMPLISHED TODAY?
_____
_____
_____
_____
_____
_____
_____
_____

HEALTH CHECK

☐ ☐ ☐ ☐ ☐ ☐ ☐   HOW MANY CUPS OF WATER DID YOU DRINK?

☐ YES   ☐ NO   DID YOU EXERCISE TODAY?
(a 15-20 min. walk counts)

WHAT ARE YOU THE MOST PROUD OF TODAY?

FRIDAY

DATE : ____ ____ ____

WHAT'S ONE THING YOU'RE GRATEFUL FOR?

_____
_____
_____

> ❝ Never waste valuable time, or mental peace of mind, on the affairs of others—that is too high a price to pay. ❞
> -Robert Greene, The 48 Laws of Power

LIST 3 MICRO GOALS YOU CAN TACKLE TODAY

1. _____
MICRO GOAL
_____
_____
_____
_____

2. _____
MICRO GOAL
_____
_____
_____
_____

3. _____
MICRO GOAL
_____
_____
_____
_____

BIG WINS / LESSONS

REFLECTION

DID YOU GET SOME OF YOUR GOALS ACCOMPLISHED TODAY?

_____
_____
_____
_____
_____
_____
_____
_____

HEALTH CHECK

▢ ▢ ▢ ▢ ▢ ▢ ▢   HOW MANY CUPS OF WATER DID YOU DRINK?

☐ YES   ☐ NO   DID YOU EXERCISE TODAY?
(a 15-20 min. walk counts)

WHAT ARE YOU THE MOST PROUD OF TODAY?

SATURDAY

DATE : ____ ____ ____

WHAT'S ONE THING YOU'RE GRATEFUL FOR?
_____
_____
_____

LIST 3 MICRO GOALS YOU CAN TACKLE TODAY

1. _____
MICRO GOAL
_____
_____
_____
_____

2. _____
MICRO GOAL
_____
_____
_____
_____

3. _____
MICRO GOAL
_____
_____
_____
_____

BIG WINS / LESSONS

DAY 62

WHAT DID YOU GET ACCOMPLISHED THE PAST 5 DAYS?

WHAT ARE SOME THINGS YOU WANT TO DO DIFFERENTLY?

SUNDAY

DATE : ____ ____ ____

WHAT'S ONE THING YOU'RE GRATEFUL FOR?

_____
_____
_____
_____
_____

> " You've got to think about the big things while you're doing small things, so that all the small things go in the right direction. " -Alvin Toffler

WHAT ARE 3 THINGS YOU CAN DO TODAY TO PREPARE FOR A SUCCESSFUL WEEK?

1. _____
_____
_____
_____

2. _____
_____
_____
_____

3. _____
_____
_____
_____

WHAT DID YOU GET ACCOMPLISHED THE PAST 5 DAYS?

_____
_____
_____
_____
_____
_____
_____
_____
_____
_____
_____
_____
_____
_____
_____

WHAT ARE SOME THINGS YOU WANT TO DO DIFFERENTLY?

_____
_____
_____
_____
_____
_____
_____
_____
_____
_____
_____
_____
_____
_____
_____
_____
_____
_____
_____
_____

MONDAY

DATE : ____ ____ ____

"Opportunities don't happen. You create them." -Chris Grosser

WHAT'S ONE THING YOU'RE GRATEFUL FOR?
_____
_____

LIST 3 MICRO GOALS YOU CAN TACKLE TODAY

1. _____

MICRO GOAL
_____
_____
_____
_____

2. _____

MICRO GOAL
_____
_____
_____
_____

3. _____

MICRO GOAL
_____
_____
_____
_____

BIG WINS / LESSONS

REFLECTION

DID YOU GET SOME OF YOUR GOALS ACCOMPLISHED TODAY?
_____
_____
_____
_____
_____
_____
_____
_____
_____

HEALTH CHECK

☐ ☐ ☐ ☐ ☐ ☐ ☐   HOW MANY CUPS OF WATER DID YOU DRINK?

☐   ☐   DID YOU EXERCISE TODAY?
YES NO (a 15-20 min. walk counts)

WHAT ARE YOU THE MOST PROUD OF TODAY?

TUESDAY

DATE : ___ ___ ___

WHAT'S ONE THING YOU'RE GRATEFUL FOR?

_____
_____
_____

> " The future belongs to those who learn more skills and combine them in creative ways. " - *Robert Greene*

LIST 3 MICRO GOALS YOU CAN TACKLE TODAY

1. _____
MICRO GOAL

2. _____
MICRO GOAL

3. _____
MICRO GOAL

BIG WINS / LESSONS

DAY 65

REFLECTION

DID YOU GET SOME OF YOUR GOALS ACCOMPLISHED TODAY?

_____
_____
_____
_____
_____
_____
_____
_____
_____

HEALTH CHECK

HOW MANY CUPS OF WATER DID YOU DRINK?

☐ YES ☐ NO

DID YOU EXERCISE TODAY?
(a 15-20 min. walk counts)

WHAT ARE YOU THE MOST PROUD OF TODAY?

WEDNESDAY

DATE : ___ ___ ___

WHAT'S ONE THING YOU'RE GRATEFUL FOR?
_____
_____
_____

LIST 3 MICRO GOALS YOU CAN TACKLE TODAY

1. _____
MICRO GOAL
_____
_____
_____
_____

2. _____
MICRO GOAL
_____
_____
_____
_____

3. _____
MICRO GOAL
_____
_____
_____
_____

BIG WINS / LESSONS

DAY 66

NOTES / IDEAS

THURSDAY

DATE : ____ ____ ____

"Only I can change my life. No one can do it for me." -Carol Burnett

WHAT'S ONE THING YOU'RE GRATEFUL FOR?
_____
_____

LIST 3 MICRO GOALS YOU CAN TACKLE TODAY

1. _____
MICRO GOAL

2. _____
MICRO GOAL

3. _____
MICRO GOAL

BIG WINS / LESSONS

REFLECTION

DID YOU GET SOME OF YOUR GOALS ACCOMPLISHED TODAY?
_____
_____
_____
_____
_____
_____
_____
_____
_____

HEALTH CHECK

HOW MANY CUPS OF WATER DID YOU DRINK?

☐ YES ☐ NO

DID YOU EXERCISE TODAY?
(a 15-20 min. walk counts)

WHAT ARE YOU THE MOST PROUD OF TODAY?

FRIDAY

DATE : ____ ____ ____

WHAT'S ONE THING YOU'RE GRATEFUL FOR?

_____
_____
_____

> " I hated every minute of training, but I said, 'Don't quit. Suffer now and live the rest of your life as a champion. " *-Muhammad Ali*

LIST 3 MICRO GOALS YOU CAN TACKLE TODAY

1. _____
MICRO GOAL

2. _____
MICRO GOAL

3. _____
MICRO GOAL

BIG WINS / LESSONS

DAY 68

REFLECTION

DID YOU GET SOME OF YOUR GOALS ACCOMPLISHED TODAY?
___
___
___
___
___
___
___
___
___

HEALTH CHECK

☐ ☐ ☐ ☐ ☐ ☐ ☐   HOW MANY CUPS OF WATER DID YOU DRINK?

☐ YES   ☐ NO   DID YOU EXERCISE TODAY?
(a 15-20 min. walk counts)

WHAT ARE YOU THE MOST PROUD OF TODAY?

SATURDAY

DATE : ___ ___ ___

WHAT'S ONE THING YOU'RE GRATEFUL FOR?

_____
_____
_____

LIST 3 MICRO GOALS YOU CAN TACKLE TODAY

1. _____
MICRO GOAL

2. _____
MICRO GOAL

3. _____
MICRO GOAL

BIG WINS / LESSONS

WHAT DID YOU GET ACCOMPLISHED THE PAST 5 DAYS?

WHAT ARE SOME THINGS YOU WANT TO DO DIFFERENTLY?

SUNDAY

DATE : ____ ____ ____

WHAT'S ONE THING YOU'RE GRATEFUL FOR?

_____
_____
_____
_____

> If you always put limit on everything you do, physical or anything else. It will spread into your work and into your life. There are no limits. There are only plateaus, and you must not stay there, you must go beyond them. -Bruce Lee

WHAT ARE 3 THINGS YOU CAN DO TODAY TO PREPARE FOR A SUCCESSFUL WEEK?

1. _____
_____
_____
_____
_____

2. _____
_____
_____
_____
_____

3. _____
_____
_____
_____
_____

DAY 70

WHAT DID YOU GET ACCOMPLISHED THE PAST 5 DAYS?

WHAT ARE SOME THINGS YOU WANT TO DO DIFFERENTLY?

MONDAY

DATE : ____ ____ ____

"All you need is the plan, the road map, and the courage to press on to your destination." -Earl Nightingale

WHAT'S ONE THING YOU'RE GRATEFUL FOR?

_____
_____

LIST 3 MICRO GOALS YOU CAN TACKLE TODAY

1. _____
MICRO GOAL

2. _____
MICRO GOAL

3. _____
MICRO GOAL

BIG WINS / LESSONS

DAY 71

REFLECTION

DID YOU GET SOME OF YOUR GOALS ACCOMPLISHED TODAY?
_____
_____
_____
_____
_____
_____
_____
_____
_____

HEALTH CHECK

HOW MANY CUPS OF WATER DID YOU DRINK?

☐ YES ☐ NO

DID YOU EXERCISE TODAY?
(a 15-20 min. walk counts)

WHAT ARE YOU THE MOST PROUD OF TODAY?

TUESDAY

DATE : ____ ____ ____

WHAT'S ONE THING YOU'RE GRATEFUL FOR?

___

> " We must all suffer one of two things: the pain of discipline or the pain of regret or disappointment. " *- Jim Rohn*

LIST 3 MICRO GOALS YOU CAN TACKLE TODAY

1. _____
MICRO GOAL

2. _____
MICRO GOAL

3. _____
MICRO GOAL

BIG WINS / LESSONS

DAY 72

REFLECTION

DID YOU GET SOME OF YOUR GOALS ACCOMPLISHED TODAY?
_____
_____
_____
_____
_____
_____
_____
_____

HEALTH CHECK

HOW MANY CUPS OF WATER DID YOU DRINK?

☐ YES   ☐ NO

DID YOU EXERCISE TODAY?
(a 15-20 min. walk counts)

WHAT ARE YOU THE MOST PROUD OF TODAY?

WEDNESDAY

DATE : ____ ____ ____

WHAT'S ONE THING YOU'RE GRATEFUL FOR?
_____
_____
_____

LIST 3 MICRO GOALS YOU CAN TACKLE TODAY

1. _____
MICRO GOAL

2. _____
MICRO GOAL

3. _____
MICRO GOAL

BIG WINS / LESSONS

DAY 73

NOTES / IDEAS

THURSDAY

DATE : ____ ____ ____

"If you don't program yourself, life will program you." -Les Brown

WHAT'S ONE THING YOU'RE GRATEFUL FOR?

___

LIST 3 MICRO GOALS YOU CAN TACKLE TODAY

1. _____
MICRO GOAL

___

2. _____
MICRO GOAL

___

3. _____
MICRO GOAL

___

BIG WINS / LESSONS

DAY 74

REFLECTION

DID YOU GET SOME OF YOUR GOALS ACCOMPLISHED TODAY?

_____
_____
_____
_____
_____
_____
_____
_____
_____

HEALTH CHECK

☐ ☐ ☐ ☐ ☐ ☐ ☐ **HOW MANY CUPS OF WATER DID YOU DRINK?**

☐ YES ☐ NO **DID YOU EXERCISE TODAY?**
(a 15-20 min. walk counts)

WHAT ARE YOU THE MOST PROUD OF TODAY?

FRIDAY

DATE : ____ ____ ____

WHAT'S ONE THING YOU'RE GRATEFUL FOR?

_____
_____
_____

> ❝ How dare you settle for less when the world has made it so easy for you to be remarkable? ❞ *-Seth Godin*

LIST 3 MICRO GOALS YOU CAN TACKLE TODAY

1. _____
MICRO GOAL
_____
_____
_____
_____

2. _____
MICRO GOAL
_____
_____
_____
_____

3. _____
MICRO GOAL
_____
_____
_____
_____

BIG WINS / LESSONS

DAY 75

REFLECTION

DID YOU GET SOME OF YOUR GOALS ACCOMPLISHED TODAY?

_____
_____
_____
_____
_____
_____
_____
_____

HEALTH CHECK

HOW MANY CUPS OF WATER DID YOU DRINK?

☐ YES   ☐ NO

DID YOU EXERCISE TODAY?
(a 15-20 min. walk counts)

WHAT ARE YOU THE MOST PROUD OF TODAY?

SATURDAY

DATE : ____ ____ ____

WHAT'S ONE THING YOU'RE GRATEFUL FOR?
_____
_____
_____

LIST 3 MICRO GOALS YOU CAN TACKLE TODAY

1. _____
MICRO GOAL
_____
_____
_____
_____

2. _____
MICRO GOAL
_____
_____
_____
_____

3. _____
MICRO GOAL
_____
_____
_____
_____

BIG WINS / LESSONS

WHAT DID YOU GET ACCOMPLISHED THE PAST 5 DAYS?

WHAT ARE SOME THINGS YOU WANT TO DO DIFFERENTLY?

SUNDAY

DATE : ____ ____ ____

WHAT'S ONE THING YOU'RE GRATEFUL FOR?

___

> " Life shrinks and expands on the proportion of your willingness to take risks and try new things. " -Gary Vaynerchuk

WHAT ARE 3 THINGS YOU CAN DO TODAY TO PREPARE FOR A SUCCESSFUL WEEK?

1.

2.

3.

WHAT DID YOU GET ACCOMPLISHED THE PAST 5 DAYS?

WHAT ARE SOME THINGS YOU WANT TO DO DIFFERENTLY?

MONDAY

DATE : ____ ____ ____

"Either you run the day, or the day runs you." -Jim Rohn

WHAT'S ONE THING YOU'RE GRATEFUL FOR?
_____
_____

LIST 3 MICRO GOALS YOU CAN TACKLE TODAY

1. _____
MICRO GOAL
_____
_____
_____
_____

2. _____
MICRO GOAL
_____
_____
_____
_____

3. _____
MICRO GOAL
_____
_____
_____
_____

BIG WINS / LESSONS

DAY 78

REFLECTION

DID YOU GET SOME OF YOUR GOALS ACCOMPLISHED TODAY?
_____
_____
_____
_____
_____
_____
_____
_____
_____

HEALTH CHECK

HOW MANY CUPS OF WATER DID YOU DRINK?

☐ YES   ☐ NO

DID YOU EXERCISE TODAY?
(a 15-20 min. walk counts)

WHAT ARE YOU THE MOST PROUD OF TODAY?

TUESDAY

DATE : _____ _____ _____

WHAT'S ONE THING YOU'RE GRATEFUL FOR?
_____
_____
_____

> " Failure will never overtake me if my determination to succeed is strong enough. " -*Og Mandino*

LIST 3 MICRO GOALS YOU CAN TACKLE TODAY

1. _____
MICRO GOAL
_____
_____
_____
_____

2. _____
MICRO GOAL
_____
_____
_____
_____

3. _____
MICRO GOAL
_____
_____
_____
_____

BIG WINS / LESSONS

┌──────────────────────────────────────┐
│   │
│   │
│   │
│   │
└──────────────────────────────────────┘

DAY 79

REFLECTION

DID YOU GET SOME OF YOUR GOALS ACCOMPLISHED TODAY?
_____
_____
_____
_____
_____
_____
_____
_____
_____
_____

HEALTH CHECK

☐ ☐ ☐ ☐ ☐ ☐   HOW MANY CUPS OF WATER DID YOU DRINK?

☐ YES   ☐ NO   DID YOU EXERCISE TODAY?
(a 15-20 min. walk counts)

WHAT ARE YOU THE MOST PROUD OF TODAY?

WEDNESDAY

DATE : ____ ____ ____

WHAT'S ONE THING YOU'RE GRATEFUL FOR?
_____
_____
_____

LIST 3 MICRO GOALS YOU CAN TACKLE TODAY

1. _____
MICRO GOAL
_____
_____
_____
_____

2. _____
MICRO GOAL
_____
_____
_____
_____

3. _____
MICRO GOAL
_____
_____
_____
_____

BIG WINS / LESSONS

NOTES / IDEAS

THURSDAY

DATE : ____ ____ ____

"Life's under no obligation to give us what we expect." -Margaret Mitchell

WHAT'S ONE THING YOU'RE GRATEFUL FOR?
_____
_____
_____

LIST 3 MICRO GOALS YOU CAN TACKLE TODAY

1. _____
MICRO GOAL
_____
_____
_____
_____

2. _____
MICRO GOAL
_____
_____
_____
_____

3. _____
MICRO GOAL
_____
_____
_____
_____

BIG WINS / LESSONS

```
┌─────────────────────────────────────────────────────┐
│                                                     │
│                                                     │
│                                                     │
│                                                     │
│                                                     │
│                                                     │
└─────────────────────────────────────────────────────┘
```

DAY 81

REFLECTION

DID YOU GET SOME OF YOUR GOALS ACCOMPLISHED TODAY?

_____
_____
_____
_____
_____
_____
_____
_____

HEALTH CHECK

HOW MANY CUPS OF WATER DID YOU DRINK?

☐ YES ☐ NO

DID YOU EXERCISE TODAY?
(a 15-20 min. walk counts)

WHAT ARE YOU THE MOST PROUD OF TODAY?

FRIDAY

DATE : ____ ____ ____

WHAT'S ONE THING YOU'RE GRATEFUL FOR?
_____
_____
_____

> **❝** Someone is sitting in the shade today because someone planted a tree a long time ago. **❞** *-Warren Buffett*

LIST 3 MICRO GOALS YOU CAN TACKLE TODAY

1. _____
MICRO GOAL
_____
_____
_____
_____

2. _____
MICRO GOAL
_____
_____
_____
_____

3. _____
MICRO GOAL
_____
_____
_____
_____

BIG WINS / LESSONS

```
┌─────────────────────────────────────────────────┐
│                                                 │
│                                                 │
│                                                 │
│                                                 │
│                                                 │
└─────────────────────────────────────────────────┘
```

DAY 82

REFLECTION

DID YOU GET SOME OF YOUR GOALS ACCOMPLISHED TODAY?

_____
_____
_____
_____
_____
_____
_____
_____
_____

HEALTH CHECK

☐ ☐ ☐ ☐ ☐ ☐ ☐   **HOW MANY CUPS OF WATER DID YOU DRINK?**

☐ YES ☐ NO   **DID YOU EXERCISE TODAY?**
(a 15-20 min. walk counts)

WHAT ARE YOU THE MOST PROUD OF TODAY?

SATURDAY

DATE : ____ ____ ____

WHAT'S ONE THING YOU'RE GRATEFUL FOR?

_____
_____
_____

LIST 3 MICRO GOALS YOU CAN TACKLE TODAY

1. _____
MICRO GOAL

2. _____
MICRO GOAL

3. _____
MICRO GOAL

BIG WINS / LESSONS

WHAT DID YOU GET ACCOMPLISHED THE PAST 5 DAYS?

WHAT ARE SOME THINGS YOU WANT TO DO DIFFERENTLY?

SUNDAY

DATE : ____ ____ ____

WHAT'S ONE THING YOU'RE GRATEFUL FOR?

___

> "Being aware of your fear is smart. Overcoming it is the mark of a successful person."
> -Seth Godin

WHAT ARE 3 THINGS YOU CAN DO TODAY TO PREPARE FOR A SUCCESSFUL WEEK?

1. _____

2. _____

3. _____

WHAT DID YOU GET ACCOMPLISHED THE PAST 5 DAYS?

_____
_____
_____
_____
_____
_____
_____
_____
_____
_____
_____
_____
_____
_____

WHAT ARE SOME THINGS YOU WANT TO DO DIFFERENTLY?

_____
_____
_____
_____
_____
_____
_____
_____
_____
_____
_____
_____
_____
_____
_____
_____
_____
_____
_____

MONDAY

DATE : ____ ____ ____

"Never pass up new experiences [Scarlett], They enrich the mind."
- Rhett Butler" - Margaret Mitchell, Gone with the Wind

WHAT'S ONE THING YOU'RE GRATEFUL FOR?

_____

_____

LIST 3 MICRO GOALS YOU CAN TACKLE TODAY

1. _____

MICRO GOAL

2. _____

MICRO GOAL

3. _____

MICRO GOAL

BIG WINS / LESSONS

DAY 85

REFLECTION

DID YOU GET SOME OF YOUR GOALS ACCOMPLISHED TODAY?
___
___
___
___
___
___
___
___
___

HEALTH CHECK

HOW MANY CUPS OF WATER DID YOU DRINK?

☐ YES   ☐ NO

DID YOU EXERCISE TODAY?
(a 15-20 min. walk counts)

WHAT ARE YOU THE MOST PROUD OF TODAY?

TUESDAY

DATE : ____ ____ ____

WHAT'S ONE THING YOU'RE GRATEFUL FOR?

_____
_____
_____

> " *A disciplined mind leads to happiness, and an undisciplined mind leads to suffering.* " — *Dalai Lama XIV*

LIST 3 MICRO GOALS YOU CAN TACKLE TODAY

1. _____
MICRO GOAL
_____
_____
_____
_____

2. _____
MICRO GOAL
_____
_____
_____
_____

3. _____
MICRO GOAL
_____
_____
_____
_____

BIG WINS / LESSONS

```
┌─────────────────────────────────────────┐
│                                         │
│                                         │
│                                         │
│                                         │
│                                         │
└─────────────────────────────────────────┘
```

REFLECTION

DID YOU GET SOME OF YOUR GOALS ACCOMPLISHED TODAY?
_____
_____
_____
_____
_____
_____
_____
_____

HEALTH CHECK

☐ ☐ ☐ ☐ ☐ ☐ ☐   HOW MANY CUPS OF WATER DID YOU DRINK?

☐ YES ☐ NO   DID YOU EXERCISE TODAY?
(a 15-20 min. walk counts)

WHAT ARE YOU THE MOST PROUD OF TODAY?

WEDNESDAY

DATE : ____ ____ ____

WHAT'S ONE THING YOU'RE GRATEFUL FOR?

_____
_____
_____

LIST 3 MICRO GOALS YOU CAN TACKLE TODAY

1. _____
MICRO GOAL

2. _____
MICRO GOAL

3. _____
MICRO GOAL

BIG WINS / LESSONS

NOTES / IDEAS

THURSDAY

DATE : ____ ____ ____

"Hope is not a strategy." -Chris Voss

WHAT'S ONE THING YOU'RE GRATEFUL FOR?
_____
_____

LIST 3 MICRO GOALS YOU CAN TACKLE TODAY

1. _____
MICRO GOAL

2. _____
MICRO GOAL

3. _____
MICRO GOAL

BIG WINS / LESSONS

REFLECTION

DID YOU GET SOME OF YOUR GOALS ACCOMPLISHED TODAY?
___
___
___
___
___
___
___
___
___
___

HEALTH CHECK

HOW MANY CUPS OF WATER DID YOU DRINK?

☐ YES ☐ NO

DID YOU EXERCISE TODAY?
(a 15-20 min. walk counts)

WHAT ARE YOU THE MOST PROUD OF TODAY?

FRIDAY

DATE : ___ ___ ___

WHAT'S ONE THING YOU'RE GRATEFUL FOR?

_____
_____
_____

> 66 **Clarity comes from action, not thought.** 99 *- Marie Forleo*

LIST 3 MICRO GOALS YOU CAN TACKLE TODAY

1. _____
MICRO GOAL
_____
_____
_____
_____

2. _____
MICRO GOAL
_____
_____
_____
_____

3. _____
MICRO GOAL
_____
_____
_____
_____

BIG WINS / LESSONS

DAY 89

REFLECTION

DID YOU GET SOME OF YOUR GOALS ACCOMPLISHED TODAY?

_____
_____
_____
_____
_____
_____
_____
_____
_____

HEALTH CHECK

☐ ☐ ☐ ☐ ☐ ☐ ☐   HOW MANY CUPS OF WATER DID YOU DRINK?

☐   ☐   DID YOU EXERCISE TODAY?
YES   NO   (a 15-20 min. walk counts)

WHAT ARE YOU THE MOST PROUD OF TODAY?

SATURDAY

DATE : ____ ____ ____

WHAT'S ONE THING YOU'RE GRATEFUL FOR?

_____
_____
_____

LIST 3 MICRO GOALS YOU CAN TACKLE TODAY

1. _____
MICRO GOAL

2. _____
MICRO GOAL

3. _____
MICRO GOAL

BIG WINS / LESSONS

DAY 90

WHAT DID YOU GET ACCOMPLISHED THE PAST 5 DAYS?

WHAT ARE SOME THINGS YOU WANT TO DO DIFFERENTLY?

" *Your network is your net worth!* "
WRITE DOWN 150 PEOPLE YOU'VE MET IN THE PAST 90 DAYS

1. _____
2. _____
3. _____
4. _____
5. _____
6. _____
7. _____
8. _____
9. _____
10. _____
11. _____
12. _____
13. _____
14. _____
15. _____
16. _____
17. _____
18. _____
19. _____
20. _____
21. _____
22. _____
23. _____
24. _____
25. _____
26. _____
27. _____
28. _____
29. _____
30. _____
31. _____
32. _____
33. _____
34. _____
35. _____
36. _____
37. _____
38. _____
39. _____
40. _____
41. _____
42. _____
43. _____
44. _____
45. _____
46. _____
47. _____
48. _____
49. _____
50. _____
51. _____
52. _____
53. _____
54. _____
55. _____
56. _____
57. _____
58. _____
59. _____
60. _____
61. _____
62. _____
63. _____
64. _____
65. _____
66. _____
67. _____
68. _____
69. _____
70. _____
71. _____
72. _____
73. _____
74. _____
75. _____
76. _____
77. _____
78. _____
79. _____
80. _____
81. _____
82. _____
83. _____
84. _____
85. _____
86. _____
87. _____
88. _____
89. _____
90. _____
91. _____
92. _____
93. _____
94. _____
95. _____
96. _____
97. _____
98. _____
99. _____
100. _____
101. _____
102. _____
103. _____
104. _____
105. _____
106. _____
107. _____
108. _____
109. _____
110. _____
111. _____
112. _____
113. _____
114. _____
115. _____
116. _____
117. _____
118. _____
119. _____
120. _____
121. _____
122. _____
123. _____
124. _____
125. _____
126. _____
127. _____
128. _____
129. _____
130. _____
131. _____
132. _____
133. _____
134. _____
135. _____
136. _____
137. _____
138. _____
136. _____
137. _____
138. _____
139. _____
140. _____
141. _____
142. _____
143. _____
144. _____
145. _____
146. _____
147. _____
148. _____
149. _____
150. _____

HOW HAS YOUR CONTACT LIST TO CHANGED OR IMPROVED WITHIN THE LAST 90 DAYS?

CONGRATULATIONS YOU DID IT!

You made it through your 90 day planner. I really hope that you made the most out of these 90 days. That you really took action, that you attended networking events to meet new people, you hit the gym, and you were able to get closer to reaching your goals.

- Ericka S. Williams